Angle Classification and Measurement

6th Grade Geometry Books
Vol I
Children's Math Books

BABY PROFESSOR

EDUCATION KIDS

Speedy Publishing LLC

40 E. Main St. #1156

Newark, DE 19711

www.speedypublishing.com

Copyright 2016

ANGLE CLASSIFICATION

Classify each angle as acute, obtuse, right, or straight.

1) _____

2)  _____

3) 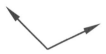 _____

4) _____

5) _____

Classify each angle as acute, obtuse, right, or straight.

6)    _____

7)    _____

8)    _____

9)   _____

10)   _____

NAME: _____

Classify each angle as acute, obtuse, right, or straight.

1) 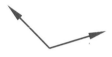 _____

2) _____

3) _____

4)  _____

5) 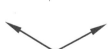 _____

Classify each angle as acute, obtuse, right, or straight.

6)   _____

7)    _____

8)   _____

9)    _____

10) 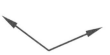   _____

Classify each angle as acute, obtuse, right, or straight.

1) _____

2) _____

3)  _____

4) _____

5) _____

Classify each angle as acute, obtuse, right, or straight.

6)  _____

7) _____

8) _____

9) _____

10) _____

Classify each angle as acute, obtuse, right, or straight.

1) _____

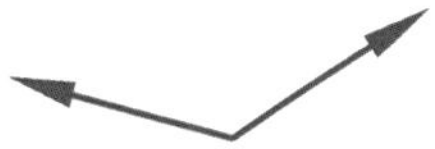

2) _____

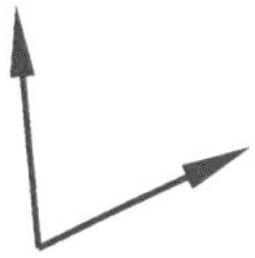

3) _____

4) _____

5) _____

Classify each angle as acute, obtuse, right, or straight.

6)   _____

7)   _____

8)  _____

9)  _____

10)   _____

NAME: _____

Classify each angle as acute, obtuse, right, or straight.

1)   _____

2)   _____

3)   _____

4)   _____

5) 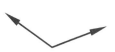 _____

Classify each angle as acute, obtuse, right, or straight.

6)  _____

7) _____

8) _____

9) _____

10) _____

NAME: _____

Classify each angle as acute, obtuse, right, or straight.

1)  _____

2) _____

3) _____

4) _____

5) _____

Classify each angle as acute, obtuse, right, or straight.

6)  _____

7) _____

8) _____

9) _____

10) _____

Classify each angle as acute, obtuse, right, or straight.

1)  _____

2) 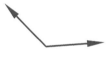 _____

3)   _____

4)   _____

5)   _____

NAME: _____

Classify each angle as acute, obtuse, right, or straight.

6)  _____

7)   _____

8)   _____

9)   _____

10)   _____

Classify each angle as acute, obtuse, right, or straight.

1) _____

2) _____

3) _____

4) _____

5) _____

Classify each angle as acute, obtuse, right, or straight.

6)    _____

7)   _____

8)   _____

9)   _____

10)   _____

NAME: _____

Classify each angle as acute, obtuse, right, or straight.

1)   _____

2)   _____

3)   _____

4)   _____

5)   _____

NAME: _____

Classify each angle as acute, obtuse, right, or straight.

6) _____

7)  _____

8)  _____

9) _____

10) _____

Classify each angle as acute, obtuse, right, or straight.

1) _____

2) _____

3) 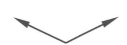 _____

4) 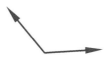 _____

5) _____

Classify each angle as acute, obtuse, right, or straight.

6) _____

7) _____

8) _____

9) _____

10) _____

Classify each angle as acute, obtuse, right, or straight.

1)  _____

2)  _____

3)   _____

4) 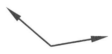 _____

5)   _____

NAME: _____

Classify each angle as acute, obtuse, right, or straight.

6) _____

7)  _____

8) _____

9)  _____

10) _____

NAME: _____

Classify each angle as acute, obtuse, right, or straight.

EXERCISE
11

1) _____

2) _____

3) _____

4) _____

5) _____

Classify each angle as acute, obtuse, right, or straight.

6)   _____

7)    _____

8)   _____

9)   _____

10)    _____

1) _____

2) _____

3)  _____

4) _____

5) 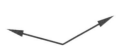 _____

Classify each angle as acute, obtuse, right, or straight.

6)  _____

7) 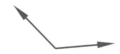 _____

8) _____

9)  _____

10)  _____

NAME: _____

Classify each angle as acute, obtuse, right, or straight.

1) _____

2) _____

3) _____

4) _____

5) _____

NAME: _____

Classify each angle as acute, obtuse, right, or straight.

6) _____

7) _____

8) _____

9) _____

10) _____

Classify each angle as acute, obtuse, right, or straight.

1) _____

2) _____

3) _____

4) _____

5) _____

NAME: _____

Classify each angle as acute, obtuse, right, or straight.

6)  _____

7)   _____

8)  _____

9)   _____

10) 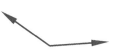 _____

Classify each angle as acute, obtuse, right, or straight.

1) _____

2)  _____

3)  _____

4) _____

5) _____

Classify each angle as acute, obtuse, right, or straight.

6)  _____

7)  _____

8)  _____

9) _____

10) 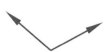 _____

MISSING ANGLE MEASUREMENT

NAME: _____

Find the missing angle measurement in
each set of complementary angles.

1)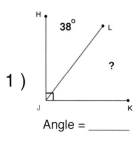

Angle = _____

2)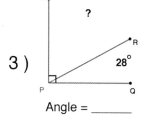

Angle = _____

3)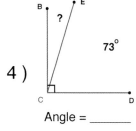

Angle = _____

4)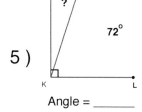

Angle = _____

5)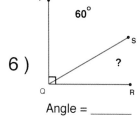

Angle = _____

6)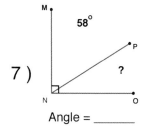

Angle = _____

7)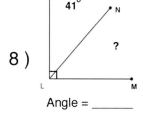

Angle = _____

8)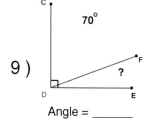

Angle = _____

9)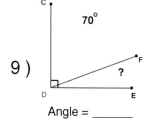

Angle = _____

NAME: _____

Find the missing angle measurement in
each set of complementary angles.

1)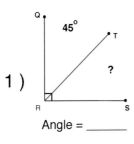

Angle = _____

2)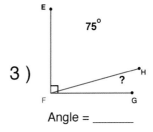

Angle = _____

3)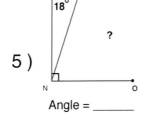

Angle = _____

4)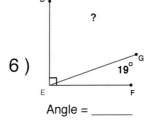

Angle = _____

5)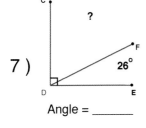

Angle = _____

6)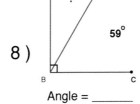

Angle = _____

7)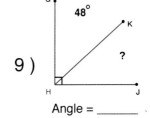

Angle = _____

8)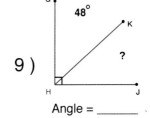

Angle = _____

9)

Angle = _____

NAME: _____

Find the missing angle measurement in
each set of complementary angles.

1)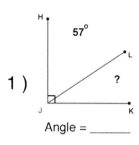

Angle = _____

2)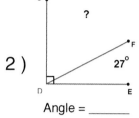

Angle = _____

3)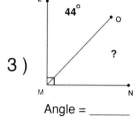

Angle = _____

4)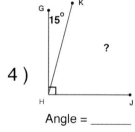

Angle = _____

5)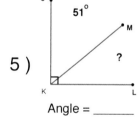

Angle = _____

6)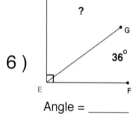

Angle = _____

7)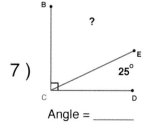

Angle = _____

8)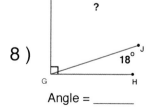

Angle = _____

9)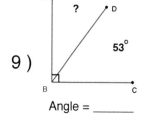

Angle = _____

NAME: _____

Find the missing angle measurement in
each set of complementary angles.

1)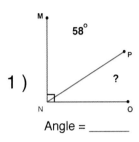

Angle = _____

2)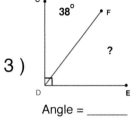

Angle = _____

3)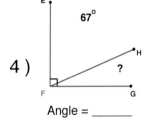

Angle = _____

4)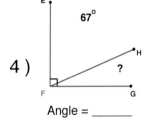

Angle = _____

5)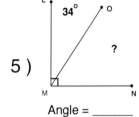

Angle = _____

6)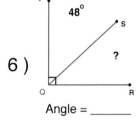

Angle = _____

7)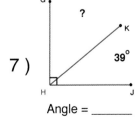

Angle = _____

8)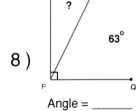

Angle = _____

9)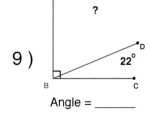

Angle = _____

NAME: _____

Find the missing angle measurement in
each set of complementary angles.

1)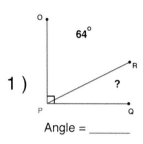

Angle = _____

2)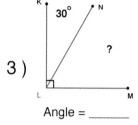

Angle = _____

3)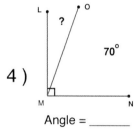

Angle = _____

4)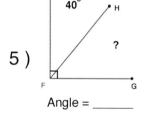

Angle = _____

5)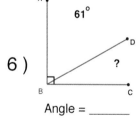

Angle = _____

6)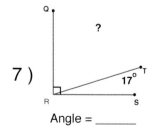

Angle = _____

7)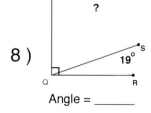

Angle = _____

8)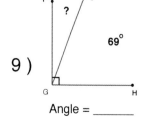

Angle = _____

9)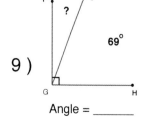

Angle = _____

NAME: _____

Find the missing angle measurement in
each set of complementary angles.

1)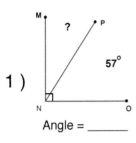

Angle = _____

2)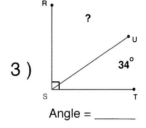

Angle = _____

3)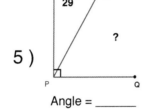

Angle = _____

4)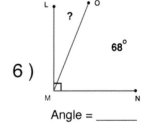

Angle = _____

5)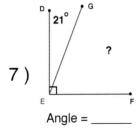

Angle = _____

6)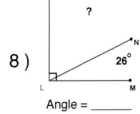

Angle = _____

7)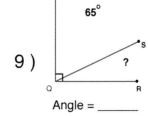

Angle = _____

8)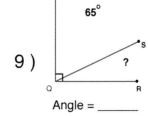

Angle = _____

9)

Angle = _____

NAME: _____

Find the missing angle measurement in
each set of complementary angles.

1)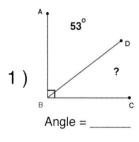

Angle = _____

2)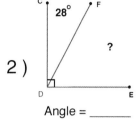

Angle = _____

3)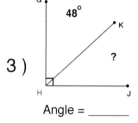

Angle = _____

4)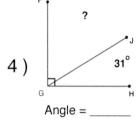

Angle = _____

5)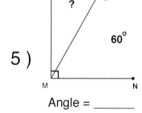

Angle = _____

6)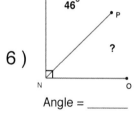

Angle = _____

7)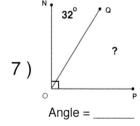

Angle = _____

8)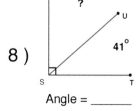

Angle = _____

9)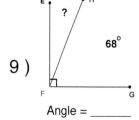

Angle = _____

NAME: _____

Find the missing angle measurement in
each set of complementary angles.

1)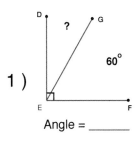

Angle = _____

2)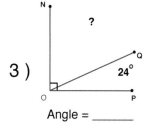

Angle = _____

3)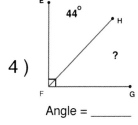

Angle = _____

4)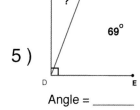

Angle = _____

5)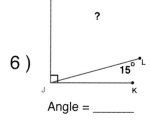

Angle = _____

6)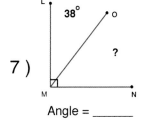

Angle = _____

7)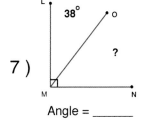

Angle = _____

8)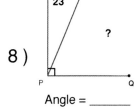

Angle = _____

9)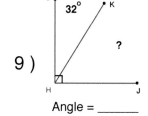

Angle = _____

NAME: _____

Find the missing angle measurement in
each set of complementary angles.

1)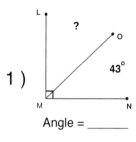

Angle = _____

2)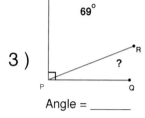

Angle = _____

3)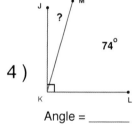

Angle = _____

4)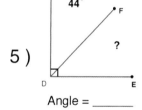

Angle = _____

5)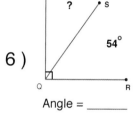

Angle = _____

6)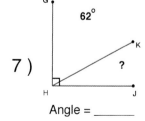

Angle = _____

7)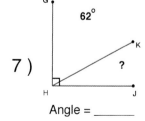

Angle = _____

8)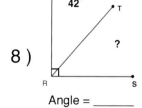

Angle = _____

9)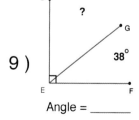

Angle = _____

NAME: _____

Find the missing angle measurement in
each set of complementary angles.

1)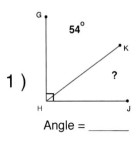

Angle = _____

2)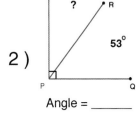

Angle = _____

3)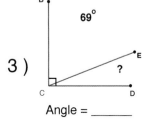

Angle = _____

4)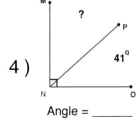

Angle = _____

5)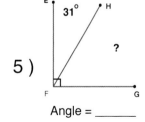

Angle = _____

6)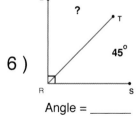

Angle = _____

7)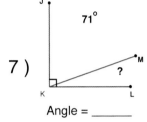

Angle = _____

8)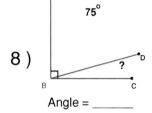

Angle = _____

9)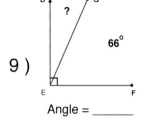

Angle = _____

ANSWERS

ANGLE
CLASSIFICATION

EXERCISE 1

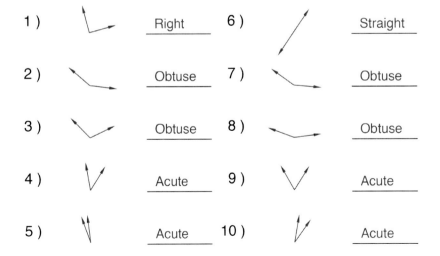

1)   Right

2)   Obtuse

3)   Obtuse

4)   Acute

5)   Acute

6)   Straight

7)   Obtuse

8)   Obtuse

9)   Acute

10)   Acute

EXERCISE 2

1) <u>Obtuse</u> 6) <u>Acute</u>

2) <u>Acute</u> 7) <u>Right</u>

3) <u>Acute</u> 8) <u>Acute</u>

4) <u>Straight</u> 9) <u>Obtuse</u>

5) <u>Obtuse</u> 10) <u>Obtuse</u>

EXERCISE 3

1) <u>Acute</u> 6) <u>Obtuse</u>

2) <u>Right</u> 7) <u>Acute</u>

3) <u>Straight</u> 8) <u>Obtuse</u>

4) <u>Acute</u> 9) <u>Acute</u>

5) <u>Obtuse</u> 10) <u>Obtuse</u>

EXERCISE 4

1)   Obtuse   6)   Acute

2)   Acute   7)   Acute

3)   Acute   8)   Obtuse

4)   Straight   9)   Obtuse

5)   Obtuse   10)   Right

EXERCISE 5

1)   Right   6)   Obtuse

2)   Acute   7)   Obtuse

3)   Acute   8)   Straight

4)   Acute   9)   Acute

5)   Obtuse   10)   Obtuse

EXERCISE 6

1) _Straight_   6) _Obtuse_

2) _Acute_   7) _Obtuse_

3) _Acute_   8) _Obtuse_

4) _Acute_   9) _Obtuse_

5) _Right_   10) _Acute_

EXERCISE 7

1) _Right_   6) _Obtuse_

2) _Obtuse_   7) _Obtuse_

3) _Acute_   8) _Straight_

4) _Acute_   9) _Acute_

5) _Acute_   10) _Obtuse_

EXERCISE 8

1)   Obtuse   6)   Acute

2)   Right   7)   Obtuse

3)   Obtuse   8)   Straight

4)   Acute   9)   Acute

5)   Obtuse   10)   Acute

EXERCISE 9

1)   Acute   6)   Obtuse

2)   Acute   7)   Right

3)   Obtuse   8)   Straight

4)   Obtuse   9)   Obtuse

5)   Acute   10)   Acute

EXERCISE 10

1) _____ Obtuse   6) _____ Acute

2) _____ Obtuse   7) _____ Straight

3) _____ Acute   8) _____ Right

4) _____ Obtuse   9) _____ Obtuse

5) _____ Acute   10) _____ Acute

EXERCISE 11

1) _____ Obtuse   6) _____ Acute

2) _____ Obtuse   7) _____ Obtuse

3) _____ Acute   8) _____ Acute

4) _____ Right   9) _____ Acute

5) _____ Obtuse   10) _____ Straight

EXERCISE 12

1)   Acute _____   6)   Right _____

2)   Acute _____   7)   Obtuse _____

3)   Straight _____   8)   Acute _____

4)   Acute _____   9)   Obtuse _____

5)   Obtuse _____   10)   Obtuse _____

EXERCISE 13

1)   Obtuse _____   6)   Obtuse _____

2)   Right _____   7)   Obtuse _____

3)   Acute _____   8)   Straight _____

4)   Acute _____   9)   Acute _____

5)   Obtuse _____   10)   Acute _____

EXERCISE 14

1) _____ Obtuse

2) _____ Acute

3) _____ Acute

4) _____ Obtuse

5) _____ Right

6) _____ Straight

7) _____ Acute

8) _____ Obtuse

9) _____ Acute

10) _____ Obtuse

EXERCISE 15

1) _____ Right

2) _____ Obtuse

3) _____ Obtuse

4) _____ Acute

5) _____ Acute

6) _____ Straight

7) _____ Acute

8) _____ Obtuse

9) _____ Acute

10) _____ Obtuse

MISSING ANGLE MEASUREMENT

1)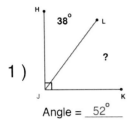

Angle = _52°_

2)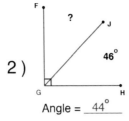

Angle = _44°_

3)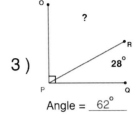

Angle = _62°_

4)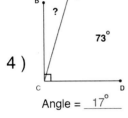

Angle = _17°_

5)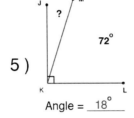

Angle = _18°_

6)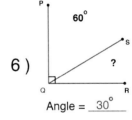

Angle = _30°_

7)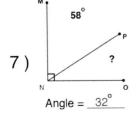

Angle = _32°_

8)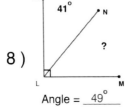

Angle = _49°_

9)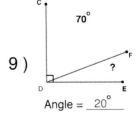

Angle = _20°_

EXERCISE 2

1)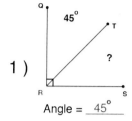

Angle = _45°_

2)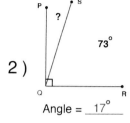

Angle = _17°_

3)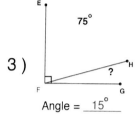

Angle = _15°_

4)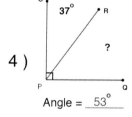

Angle = _53°_

5)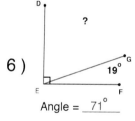

Angle = _72°_

6)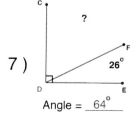

Angle = _71°_

7)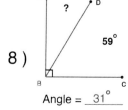

Angle = _64°_

8)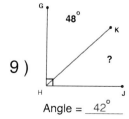

Angle = _31°_

9)

Angle = _42°_

EXERCISE 3

1)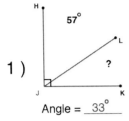

Angle = _33°_

2)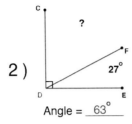

Angle = _63°_

3)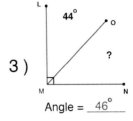

Angle = _46°_

4)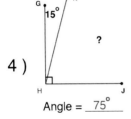

Angle = _75°_

5)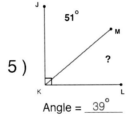

Angle = _39°_

6)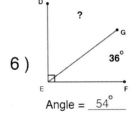

Angle = _54°_

7)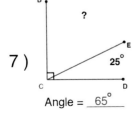

Angle = _65°_

8)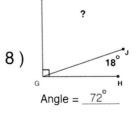

Angle = _72°_

9)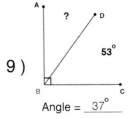

Angle = _37°_

EXERCISE 4

1)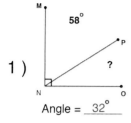
Angle = 32°

2)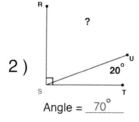
Angle = 70°

3)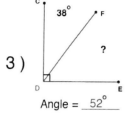
Angle = 52°

4)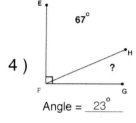
Angle = 23°

5)
Angle = 56°

6)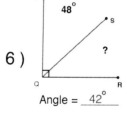
Angle = 42°

7)
Angle = 51°

8)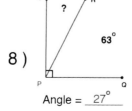
Angle = 27°

9)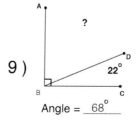
Angle = 68°

EXERCISE 5

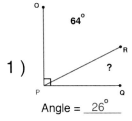

1)

Angle = __26°__

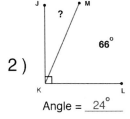

2)

Angle = __24°__

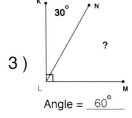

3)

Angle = __60°__

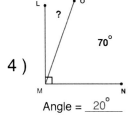

4)

Angle = __20°__

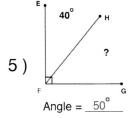

5)

Angle = __50°__

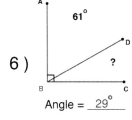

6)

Angle = __29°__

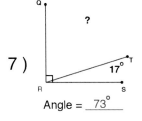

7)

Angle = __73°__

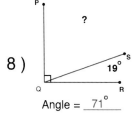

8)

Angle = __71°__

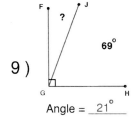

9)

Angle = __21°__

1)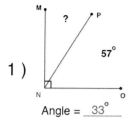

Angle = _33°_

2)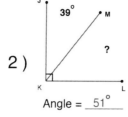

Angle = _51°_

3)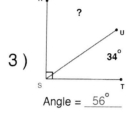

Angle = _56°_

4)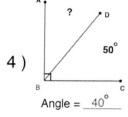

Angle = _40°_

5)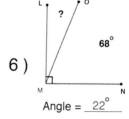

Angle = _61°_

6)

Angle = _22°_

7)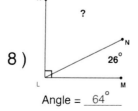

Angle = _69°_

8)

Angle = _64°_

9)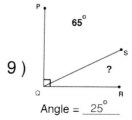

Angle = _25°_

EXERCISE 7

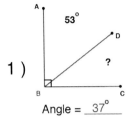

1)   Angle = _37°_

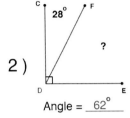

2)   Angle = _62°_

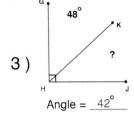

3)   Angle = _42°_

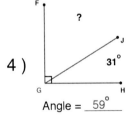

4)   Angle = _59°_

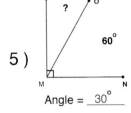

5)   Angle = _30°_

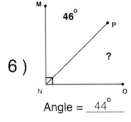

6)   Angle = _44°_

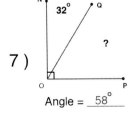

7)   Angle = _58°_

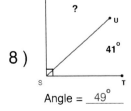

8)   Angle = _49°_

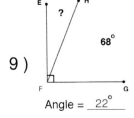

9)   Angle = _22°_

1)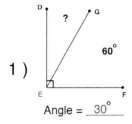
Angle = __30°__

2)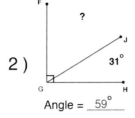
Angle = __59°__

3)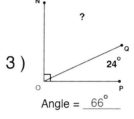
Angle = __66°__

4)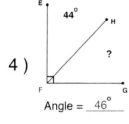
Angle = __46°__

5)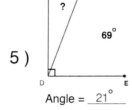
Angle = __21°__

6)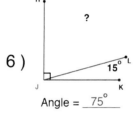
Angle = __75°__

7)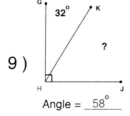
Angle = __52°__

8)
Angle = __67°__

9)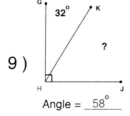
Angle = __58°__

EXERCISE 9

1)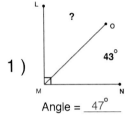

Angle = __47°__

2)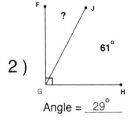

Angle = __29°__

3)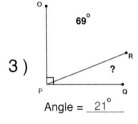

Angle = __21°__

4)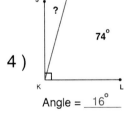

Angle = __16°__

5)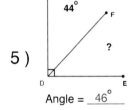

Angle = __46°__

6)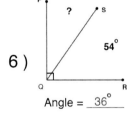

Angle = __36°__

7)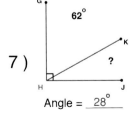

Angle = __28°__

8)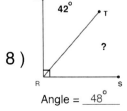

Angle = __48°__

9)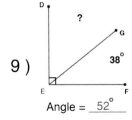

Angle = __52°__

EXERCISE 10

1)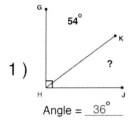

Angle = 36°

2)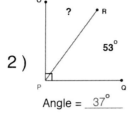

Angle = 37°

3)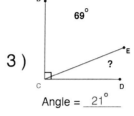

Angle = 21°

4)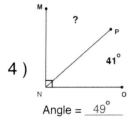

Angle = 49°

5)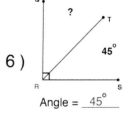

Angle = 59°

6)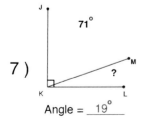

Angle = 45°

7)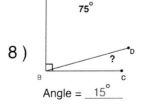

Angle = 19°

8)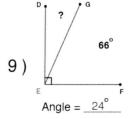

Angle = 15°

9)

Angle = 24°